MW01690638

# How the BIBLE Came to You

SHIRA SORKO-RAM

CO-FOUNDER OF MAOZ ISRAEL MINISTRIES

Copyright 2021 by:
Maoz Israel Publishers, Inc.
PO Box 535788
Grand Prairie, TX 75053
214.677.0560
info@maozisrael.org
www.maozisrael.org
www.istandwithisrael.com

All rights reserved. This book or parts thereof may not be reproduced in any form without prior written permission from the publisher.

Scripture references taken from:

*(NLT) New Living Translation*
Scripture quotations marked (NLT) are taken from the Holy Bible, New Living Translation, copyright ©1996, 2004, 2015 by Tyndale House Foundation. Used by permission of Tyndale House Publishers, Carol Stream, Illinois 60188. All rights reserved.

*(NASB) New American Standard Bible*
Scripture taken from the NEW AMERICAN STANDARD BIBLE, Copyright 1960, 1962, 1963 1968, 1971, 1972, 1973, 1975, 1977, 1995 by The Lockman Foundation. All rights reserved. Used by permission.

*(NKJV) New King James Version*
Scriptures marked NKJV are taken from the NEW KING JAMES VERSION (NKJV). Copyright© 1982 by Thomas Nelson, Inc. Used by permission. All rights reserved.

*(NIV) New International Version*
The New International Version (NIV) is an English translation of the Bible first published in 1978 by Biblica (formerly the International Bible Society). The NIV is published by Zondervan in the United States and Hodder & Stoughton in the UK. Used by Permission. All rights reserved worldwide.

ISBN 978-965-7677-61-2

Printed in the United States of America

Cover design by Jose Lopez
Interior layout by Sheila Fredrickson

# PRAISE FOR "HOW THE BIBLE CAME TO YOU"

I have been friends with Ari and Shira Sorko-Ram for more than 30 years and have ministered with them around the world. They know the importance of the Word of God and what it means in our lives. I love how Shira has taken her love and passion for God's Word and written this beautiful book explaining how the Bible came to us and the impact it has had on the nations and kingdoms of this world. You are sure to gain a deeper understanding and appreciation of the Bible you read every day.

*— Robert Morris*
*Senior Pastor, Gateway Church*
*Bestselling Author of The Blessed Life, Beyond Blessed, and Take the Day Off*

---

From the moment I picked up this little book and began to read, I felt the Lord convicting me to get back into a pattern of daily Bible reading. If you desire to hear God's voice, discern His will or are seeking divine guidance, you must spend time each day in His word. Take a few minutes to read *How the Bible Came to You* and you'll gain a new appreciation for the greatest book ever written.

*— Jonathan Bernis*
*Host of Jewish Voice Television Program*

---

Shira Sorko-Ram has been feasting on the Word of God for decades, and she shares her infectious love for the

Word in this informative book. We have such instant access to the Scriptures today that we can easily take them for granted. That's why it is so important to be reminded of the importance the Word of God played in Israel's history and the early church. It's also important to remember that having the Scriptures translated into modern languages cost many people their lives. That's why we must cherish the Word of God, which is exactly what Shira's book will help us to do.

*— Dr. Michael L. Brown,*
*Host of the Line of Fire broadcast,*
*Author of many books such as Answering Jewish Objections to Jesus: Theological Objections Vol. 2*

---

Shira Sorko-Ram believes the Bible. Period. We have been friends and coworkers for two decades. After I immigrated to Israel I had a crisis of faith. The cost of living here is very high and my support wasn't. I considered going back to America.

Shira boldly told me, "You pray and decide, but if you decide to stay, then don't ask the question again. It is settled." When she said that, a gift of faith rose up in me and I have never since questioned whether or not God wants us in Israel. Shira knows how to take hold of God's word and stand. She developed that kind of faith over many years of faithful engagement with the Holy Spirit through the Word of God. Let this book reveal to you the miracle that is God's Word.

*— Ron Cantor*
*President, Shelanu TV and Messiah's Mandate*

# Contents

FOREWORD
God's Word and Us ........................................ vii

CHAPTER 1
*Israel Couldn't Live Without It*
The Power of God's Word ........................................ 1

CHAPTER 2
*From Ezra to the Pharisees*
The Rise and Fall of the Word of God ........................................ 13

CHAPTER 3
*From the Apostles to the Reformation*
When the Word of God Ceased to Exist ........................................ 23

CHAPTER 4
*The Reformation and the Printing Press*
The Bloody Battle to Liberate the Word of God ........................................ 35

CHAPTER 5
*The Word Comes to the German People*
The Steep Price for a Bible You Could
Actually Read ........................................ 45

Chapter 6
*William Tyndale 1494 – 1536*
The Bible Translated into English ........ 51

Chapter 7
*Pilgrims Searching for Freedom*
The Bible Arrives in the Americas ........ 59

Source Notes ........ 69

Meet Shira Sorko-Ram! ........ 73

# FOREWORD
# GOD'S WORD AND US

This foreword may seem a bit heavy. I debated whether to write it or not. The reason for my caution is that in our sincere desire to please God by perfecting our good works, we can forget that our God is indescribably full of love for us and so infinitely full of compassion and mercy.

Instead of our accuser, He is our protector and defender, our advisor and counselor. He loves us with our blemishes and wants the absolute best for us—specifically so we will be able to fulfill the purpose for which we were born! But to achieve that goal, we must learn how to hear God's voice and to detect when the enemy of our lives is attempting to deceive us and cause us to get off track.

First of all, the Bible teaches us that the closer we get to God, the more we understand how much He loves us, not how much He wants to judge us. One of my aims, lately, is to really hear God's voice more clearly than ever before.

What I've been learning is that when I get a prompting—like to stop fiddling with my iPhone and work on something important, or when I feel an urge to call or write someone, to do it immediately. I find it is making my spirit more sensitive to His guidance. But how do I know if He is speaking to me or it's only my own thoughts?

I have found the answer in regularly reading the Bible. Yes, the magnificent gift God has given me as a born-again believer is His written Word. This Word, which the Bible tells us is *alive,* will absolutely change your life—if you read it regularly.

I have found it gives me great insight to understand what happened in the past and why it happened. As a result, it gives me fundamental insights into what is about to happen as this Age comes to an end. It will do the same for you.

His Word instructs us to understand what God wants from us—personally, and nationally. Through it, we discover His ways—the things He loves and the things He hates. It reveals to us the way to grow closer and closer in our relationship with Him. And that, my friend, is the most essential and meaningful pursuit of our entire lives. Slowly, we learn that it's not what we do, but *who* we are becoming.

As you read or listen to His Word, you will find the gap between you and the world's morality widens. Now we come to the nitty gritty. Today there are many churches where the words *repentance* and *sin* have little or no place in their messages, and, under the guise of tolerance, they proclaim that just about anything goes. Yet the Bible teaches repentance of sin by *believers* is the key to a close relationship with God and the gateway to revival.

God's people in many countries are waiting for the mighty outpouring of God's Spirit on this world which the Prophet Joel and others promised. Many prophetic voices today are affirming God's promises for revival. They also point out the evil and wickedness in the world that will be judged, culminating in the Great Tribulation.

But very few mention the need for *repentance of believers* when speaking of revival. Of course, repentance signifies that I, as a child of God, need to search my heart regularly for areas in which to seek forgiveness that will bring me closer in my relationship with God.

When His disciples asked Yeshua to show them how to pray, He emphasized the need for His followers to repent and to even pray for future protection against Satan's wiles with these words:

> ***... and forgive us our sins, as we forgive those who sin against us. And don't let us yield to temptation.*** *Luke 11:4 (NLT)*

So, what temptations should we watch out for? Again, we find the answer in the Bible. Here is an example: some of the sins Paul lists might not seem significant enough that we as believers need to repent of—strife, jealousy, outbursts of anger, disputes, dissensions, envying, etc. (Galatians 5) Or what about laziness or selfishness?

The list is pretty long. Who among us hasn't struggled with pride? Yet prideful people are not able to repent. Humble people can. In some cases, Yeshua explains how a root sin can lead to greater sin—as in anger leading to murder, or lust leading to adultery. These Bible stories warn us to guard our hearts and thoughts by being sensitive to His Holy Spirit and immediately asking God to forgive us.

The Lord explicitly told us that Israel is God's example of how He relates to us when we are obedient or disobedient. (I Corinthians 10:6) The Bible shares specific stories that spell it out. God destroyed multitudes of the children of Israel for grumbling!

Grumbling because they didn't have food in the desert! Grumbling because they didn't have water! What can we learn from this dire story? We must guard our mouth, not complain, and believe that God will hear our requests!

We are less tempted to complain when we consciously thank Him for the things we do have. But what about when we are in need? In great need? God's Word teaches that if we look to Him and hold on to the truth that God is good and that God will supply all of our needs, He will!

And what about judging? I know I am as human as the next person. It is natural for me to judge other believers.

It's often easy to see their faults. And yes, we are clearly commanded to judge immorality. (I Corinthians 5) But God tells us to keep in mind that if we judge others, God will judge us with the same standard! We know this because Yeshua said,

> ***For in the way you judge, you will be judged; and by your standard of measure, it will be measured to you.*** *Matthew 7:2 (NASB)*

But if I did not have God's Word, I wouldn't know that I'd bring judgment on myself if I judged others for the same things I do. Wow! That's heavy! I need a regular dose of God's Word—every day—to remember what pleases our Savior. Think of all the believers who don't know this commandment. Really knowing the Word of God doesn't bring condemnation; it brings us joy and gladness and appreciation of God's great love for us!

Perhaps one of the most significant insights the Bible gives us is the correlation between unanswered prayer and unforgiveness. God's Word instructs us that we must not hold a grudge in our heart against anyone, period! One of the most powerful Scriptures in the Bible promises that whatever we say, according to His will, God will give it to us. The one condition is that we forgive:

> ***For assuredly, I say to you, whoever says to this mountain, 'Be removed and be cast into the sea,' and does not doubt in his heart, but believes that those things he says will be done, he will have whatever he says.***

> ***Therefore, I say to you, whatever things you ask when you pray, believe that you receive them, and you will have them.***
>
> ***And whenever you stand praying, if you have anything against anyone, forgive him, that your Father in heaven may also forgive you your trespasses.***
>
> ***But if you do not forgive, neither will your Father in heaven forgive your trespasses.***
> *Mark 11:23-25 (NKJV)*

The Word of God gives us a world view as to how God sees things. As we humbly explore God's Word daily, we have His standards and loving wisdom before our eyes to keep us from deception. That is why I read the Bible through every year.

In this book I will lay out the historical connection between the availability of God's Word since it was written and the rise and fall of nations and kingdoms. Unlike past generations before us, today you can purchase many different Bibles published for whomever wants to read the Bible through in one, two or three years.

I recommend you get one for yourself if you are looking for a way to have a regular routine for reading your Bible. Yes! It will change your life.

## CHAPTER 1

*Israel Couldn't Live Without It*

# The Power of God's Word

Have you ever thought about how God dealt with his people before there was the written Word of God? Enoch had no Bible. Neither did Noah—or Abraham, Isaac and Jacob. Our Bible teaches us that though these men didn't have the written Word, God spoke to them face to face.

But the Bible doesn't say anything about God speaking to the children of Israel over the long period they were slaves in Egypt. Yet God was listening to their cries and knew their sorrows. And He had a plan. *(Exodus 3:7-8)*

In a world-changing moment of history, Moses appeared on the scene. By the strangest of coincidences, while a paranoid Pharaoh was attempting to decrease the number of the children of Israel by killing male babies, Moses was taken into the household of Pharaoh and raised by a royal daughter.

The importance of these circumstances cannot be overstated when we realize Egypt was one of the most advanced civilizations in the world. And Moses, as an adopted royal, received the finest education the world could offer at that time. For sure, he knew hieroglyphics.

Non-believing archeologists have long declared Moses could not have written the Torah, as no one could write Hebrew at that time. But new archeological evidence[1] may eventually put another nail in the coffin of atheistic denial. The constant flow of new archeological discoveries here in Israel continues to keep proving the Bible is, after all, true and accurate.

According to the Bible, Moses led Israel out of Egypt around 1445 B.C. And Moses spent the last 40 years of his life leading the children of Israel in the wilderness and writing down the words that God Himself dictated to him in Hebrew. The Torah—the Five Books of Moses—was immediately recognized by the people of Israel as an authorized book given to Moses by God.

And Moses read it to all the people:

> ***Then he took the Book of the Covenant and read in the hearing of the people. And they said, "All that the Lord has said we will do, and be obedient."*** *Exodus 24:7 (NKJV)*

The Scriptures suggest there were around 2,000,000[2] people who followed Moses out of Egypt. Without microphones, he obviously had to have help—a lot of help—to dispense the Word of God to these people.

By writing it down, the Torah would be able to reach unlimited numbers of Israelites. The Lord told him to select one tribe—the Levites—to serve the Lord and the people as spiritual ministers. They were to copy the scrolls of the Torah and place a copy alongside the Ark of the Covenant. (Deuteronomy 31:24-26)

It must have been an organizational challenge out in the desert to read the full Torah to all Israel! What a task!

But Moses knew the leaders of Israel had to be immersed in the Word of God in order to serve the Lord with all their hearts. In fact, Moses had commanded all future kings of Israel to write their own copy of the Law from the Levites' copy.

> ***... and [the king] shall read it all the days of his life ... that he may not turn aside from the commandment to the right hand or to the left, that he may prolong his days in his kingdom ...***
> *Deuteronomy 17:18-20 (NKJV)*

## JOSHUA

Moses' successor, Joshua, picked up the mantle to take possession of the land God promised Israel. During Joshua's 52 years[3] of leading Israel, he chose Shiloh as the spiritual center for the nation. Joshua set up the Tabernacle of Meeting there which housed the Ark of the Covenant, together with the Torah scrolls. Joshua was faithful to get the Word of God into the hearts and minds of the children of Israel.

There was not a word of all that Moses had commanded which Joshua did not read before all the assembly of Israel, with the women, the little ones, and the strangers who were living among them. (Joshua 8:35 NKJV)

Furthermore, he added his own book that carries his name, recording the events that happened after they entered the Promised Land.

And, not surprisingly, as long as Joshua and the elders of his generation were alive, Israel served the Lord. But that doesn't mean it was an easy job. As each tribe began to possess the land God had allotted them, they began moving into distant areas across the Promised Land.

## JUDGES

Here is where the difficulties really began. Over a period of nearly three centuries, twelve different judges, living in different areas, rose up mainly as military leaders to ward off attacking enemies as the Israelites conquered the land God had promised them. These leaders were not particularly spiritual ... for the most part.

As the tribes relocated to distant areas, many moved further and further away from their God. Their lives became filled with idol worship and extreme violence. A few judges such as Deborah and Gideon were godly people. Yet there seemed to be a continuing deterioration in the quality of judges, finally arriving to the likes of Samson. Warrior, yes. Man of God, no. Without strong godly leadership, reading and obeying the Torah became less and less a priority. Rampant violence, sexual sin and idol worship took over. Tribal wars cost hundreds of thousands of lives.

The sad book of Judges ends with:

> ***In those days there was no king in Israel; everyone did what was right in his own eyes.***
> *Judges 21:25 (NKJV)*

## SAMUEL

Yet there was a remnant throughout the tribes who stayed near to God. Under the leadership of the prophet Samuel, he brought order to at least part of the newly formed nation. A mighty man of God, he served his people by travelling on a circuit to three main cities—Bethel, Gilgal and Mizpah, plus his own city of Ramah—and judged Israel. As judge, he was teaching the Law of Moses and the book of Joshua to his people. Before Samuel died, he also added the books of Judges and Samuel to the written Word of God. Nevertheless, there were surely many towns and villages far away from the spiritual center of Israel. It is doubtful that every Israelite was receiving a steady diet of the Word of God.

## DAVID AND SOLOMON

The period of Kings came next. The House of Israel probably heard more Scripture during King David and Solomon's reigns than any other period since the death of

Moses. Clearly from the Scriptures, King David, though he started out as a shepherd, became an educated judge, musician, writer, poet and prophet.

David brought order to the entire priestly and Levitical tribe—all 38,000 of them! His favorite way of bringing the Word of God was through prophetic and worship songs, together with historical psalms of God's interaction with Israel through the centuries. He appointed 4,000 musicians who worshiped with song and musical instruments.

It is hard to accentuate enough how powerful his "Words of God" set to music have impacted Israel through the ages. His songs were sung or read throughout the centuries, and they carried much divine revelation in their lyrics. David was most certainly an intense student of the available books of the Bible in his generation. He loved the Word of God! The first Psalm reads:

> ***Blessed is the man... His delight is in the law of the Lord, and in His law he meditates day and night.*** *Psalm 1:1-2 (NKJV)*

David made sure the Israelites were paying tithes to the Levites under his reign so that the Levites and priests could study the written Word of God and administrate it. In Bible days, most Israelites could not read or write. But as long as the leadership—the kings, priests, Levites and prophets—were immersed in the Word of God, they would maintain a culture of godliness to their people.

Solomon's fame as a brilliant and wise king was known far and wide. It would seem, however, that as Solomon's lifestyle became more carnal, he spent less time with the Lord and His Word. He forgot the Torah scripture:

> ***Neither shall [the King] multiply wives for himself, lest his heart turn away; nor shall he greatly multiply silver and gold for himself.***
> *Deuteronomy 17:17 (NKJV)*

## THE NORTHERN KINGDOM OF ISRAEL

Because of Solomon's arrogant son who clearly lacked the wisdom of God, the kingdom was ripped apart. The Ten Tribes of Israel never had a single righteous king after that—with the partial exception of Jehu—until they were exiled to Assyria! It is safe to say, none of their twenty kings kept a copy of the authorized Word of God near them. The people had no one to teach them the Word of God.

In fact, these wicked kings of the northern Kingdom of Israel did not allow their citizens to even visit Jerusalem to worship, out of fear they might give their loyalty to the Kings of Judah. The kings of the Ten Tribes actually built walls to keep their people out of Judah, out of the place where the Word of God remained, beside the Ark of the Covenant.

Oded, a prophet in Judah, said of the Northern Kingdom of Israel:

> ***For a long time Israel has been without the true God, without a teaching priest and without law ...*** *II Chronicles 15:3 (NKJV)*

Yet there were prophets of God among the Ten Tribes during the years of the Northern Kingdom. Isaiah, Hosea, Amos and more were voices at that time. Elijah challenged the Israelites, saying,

> ***How long will you falter between two opinions? If the Lord is God, follow Him; but if Baal, follow him.*** *I Kings 18:21 (NKJV)*

But the people didn't know who to choose! Even after his great victory over the prophets of Baal, Elijah ran for his life against the incredibly wicked Jezebel, convinced he was the last believer alive. Yet God revealed to him there were 7,000 men who had not bowed to Baal. Nevertheless, the cup of wickedness continued to fill up. Such a disastrous condition could only lead to a tragic end. After less than 200 years, God had enough. The Ten Tribes went into exile, never to be heard from again.

## THE SOUTHERN KINGDOM OF JUDAH

Judah also had a total of twenty kings before Nebuchadnezzar who hauled the Judeans off to Babylon. Only a few of their rulers were righteous.

Solomon's immediate descendants were mediocre to bad: Rehoboam, Abijah, Asa. But it was the next king, Jehoshaphat, who restored Judah to a righteous, godly nation. God protected him, even when he made missteps, and protected his nation against fierce enemies. The Bible says:

> ***[Jehoshaphat sent his leaders] to teach in the cities of Judah ... So they taught in Judah and had the Book of the Law of the Lord with them; they went throughout all the cities of Judah and taught the people.***
> *II Chronicles 17:7, 9 (NKJV)*

Unfortunately, for the next 150 years, most of Judah's kings were not model ambassadors for the Lord. Some started out halfway good, and then as their power grew, they turned downright evil.

## HEZEKIAH AND JOSIAH— THE LAST RIGHTEOUS KINGS

Only two other kings, Hezekiah and Josiah, were truly godly men. Hezekiah repented of the many sins of his fathers and recognized the desolation their neglect of God and His Word had brought upon themselves. The Scriptures record:

> ***He opened the doors of the house of the Lord and repaired them.*** *II Chronicles 29:3 (NKJV)*

The Levites took all the garbage and debris out of the deserted Temple, and for eight days cleansed the place. Then Hezekiah commanded the Levites to go into the House of God with praise and worship. He was determined that the spiritual leadership of Judah would be focused on leading the people to love the Lord. He commanded his people to support the priests and Levites so

> ***they might devote themselves to the Law of the Lord.*** *II Chronicles 31:4 (NKJV)*

> ***And in every work that he began in the service of the house of God, in the law and in the commandment, to seek his God, he did it with all his heart. So he prospered.***
> *II Chronicles 31:21 (NKJV)*

Hezekiah saw revival among the people of his kingdom. But in his prosperity, even Hezekiah became proud at the end, and his son Manasseh, who succeeded him, was a complete disaster. Manasseh reigned for 55 years and was perhaps the most wicked of all the kings of Judah. Again, there was a total vacuum of the Word of the Lord. Again, the people were starving. Remarkably, towards the end of his life and after he had been imprisoned by the King of Syria, he repented of his terrible sins, and God heard him. But the horrific damage he had done to his nation was unredeemable.

Even though the cup of wickedness was seemingly full, God did not yet destroy the Jewish nation. Instead, He raised up Manasseh's grandson, Josiah, who became the godliest of all the kings of Judah after David! (Perhaps he had a godly mother?) Josiah became king at eight years of age. At the age of 16, he began to seek "the God of his father David." He tore down every idol he could find. At age 26, he decided to make repairs to the Temple.

As the High Priest Hilkiah was once again cleaning the Temple, he found the "Book of the Law of the Lord given by Moses." Josiah was shocked at what he read and tore his clothes.

> ***Go, inquire of the Lord for me, and for those who are left in Israel and Judah, concerning the words of the book that is found; for great is the wrath of the Lord that is poured out on us, because our fathers have not kept the word of the Lord, to do according to all that is written in this book.***
> *II Chronicles 34:21 (NKJV)*

There was a great revival during his reign. Josiah literally cleansed the country of all the abominations the children of Israel had served. The Scripture states:

> ***All his days they did not depart from following the Lord God of their fathers.***
> *II Chronicles 34:33b (NKJV)*

Tragically, Josiah was killed in battle at age 39 after ruling for 31 years. Three of Josiah's sons and one grandson ruled for the next 22 years and six months. Alas, each was more evil than the last. II Chronicles 36:14 records that under these wicked kings, the leaders and priests ***"transgressed more and more, and defiled the house of God...until there was no remedy."*** *(NKJV)* Jeremiah, the weeping prophet, and others tried desperately to warn the four descendants of Josiah, but to no avail. The Kingdom of Judah had lasted some 325 years. Now it was the end of all Israel. Little by little, exiles were hauled off to Babylon.[4] By the end, the country was so decimated from the sword, famine and disease that Nebuchadnezzar found only 4,600 Jews worth taking into exile.[5]

## TRUE PROPHETS IN EXILE

Yet there were still strong Jewish followers of the one true God. The priest, Ezekiel, who was deported to Babylon with the last king, Zedekiah, publicly prophesied and wrote a book of his visions—as to why disaster had overtaken Israel. Daniel, apparently from the royal line of the kings of Judah, and his three friends kept their intimate relationship with God, even though it almost cost them their lives. They clearly had access to the Law of Moses and the book of Jeremiah—likely all the written books until then. Daniel confessed his sins and the sins of his people as he quoted the commandments and curses in the Torah. He prayed diligently because *he read in the Book of Jeremiah* the Jewish people would return to their homeland in 70 years. There was still HOPE!

The testimony of the entire Old Testament is consistent: When the government and spiritual leaders of Israel served God and were providing their citizens with the Word of God, their nation prospered—every time.

When the children of Israel did not have the Scriptures and godly leadership, they fell back into sin, and their nation declined—and both were ultimately destroyed. Every time. Israel is our example of how God deals with individuals and with nations. All the time.

## CHAPTER 2

*From Ezra to the Pharisees*

# THE RISE AND FALL OF THE WORD OF GOD

It was 597 B.C.—the year of the first forced march of Jews exiled to Babylon. That year the Kingdom of Judah disappeared from the map. All Israel had left was a prophecy of hope by Jeremiah—that in 70 years, God would free them from their Babylonian exile and bring them back to their homeland.

> ***This is what the Lord says: "When seventy years are completed for Babylon, I will come to you and fulfill my good promise to bring you back to this place."*** *Jeremiah 29:10 (NIV)*

Then some 68 years later, a Persian King, Cyrus, conquered Babylon. God "stirred up his spirit" to decree that Jews could return home to Israel to rebuild their Temple.

Only 43,000 Jews were ready to leave Babylon. The tribe of Levites who were supposed to be the spiritual leaders of the Jewish community had fragmented. Many Jews had assimilated and intermarried. They had traded Hebrew for Aramaic, the language of Babylon, and were doing well in both business and government. Hadn't Jeremiah told them to settle in for the long haul, build houses and bless Babylon? Certainly, life was better in the diaspora than in desolate Judea. The Persians ruled, but overall, they were amiable towards their Jewish citizens who were scattered across the empire.

For those who did make the trek back to Israel, lack of strong spiritual leadership, poverty, scarcity of food and endless enemies kept them from any real economic progress. So God sent Haggai and Zachariah to encourage the rebuilding of the Temple. It would still take another 20+ years to finish.

## EZRA THE SCRIBE

And then, some 80 years later, Ezra arrived in Jerusalem. It was Ezra who made the strongest long-term spiritual impact on the struggling returnees. In 458 B.C. he brought with him another 1,800 priests, Levites and musicians, along with their families. Understand that when God spoke the promise of 70 years through Jeremiah, it did not at all mean that the Israelites' return to Israel would flow smoothly without complications and obstacles.

First of all, these returnees were not particularly dedicated children of God. Many had intermarried with the heathen. The people clearly knew little of the Law of Moses and God's commandments. The few Levites who had immigrated earlier to minister to the community's spiritual needs had no choice but to leave the ministry and earn a living, because the people were not paying their tithes. Ezra was determined to turn things around by bringing back the Word of God to his unenlightened countrymen.

> ***This Ezra came up from Babylon; and he was a skilled scribe in the Law of Moses ... for Ezra had prepared his heart to seek the Law of the Lord, and to do it, and to teach statutes and ordinances in Israel.*** *Ezra 7:6, 10 (NKJV)*

## NEEDED: A GODLY POLITICAL LEADER

Yet in the chaos, poverty and uncertainty, Ezra, perhaps the more scholarly type, was not able by himself to bring the people to true repentance and spiritual wellbeing. It was clear the Jewish people needed two essentials to create a godly nation: good civil government and spiritual leaders teaching the Word of God.

Heaven sent such a man. After Nehemiah arrived to become governor (without pay) and organized the people, they built a wall around the city to protect them from constant enemy attacks. When Israel had the combination of Nehemiah governing, Ezra teaching and the Levites worshipping (with women singers!)—revival broke out!

The whole community worshiped, celebrating with joy God's holidays and ***day by day, from the first day until***

***the last day, he [Ezra] read from the Book of the law of God.*** *Nehemiah 8:18 (NKJV)*

However, when Governor Nehemiah had to leave Israel at the request of the King for a short time, he returned to Israel only to find his people had reverted to their old lifestyle—intermarrying, not paying tithes to the Levites, and desecrating the Sabbath. The intrepid Nehemiah again organized the people, appointed two large choirs of musicians to worship and brought in Ezra, again, to teach the Law of God. As a lover of the Word of God, Ezra created a pattern of reading the Books of the Bible for generations of Jews to come—until today.

But then the prophetic Word from the mouth of God became silent for four centuries. The Levites faded away, and different spiritual leaders rose to reshape the Jewish religion according to their own understanding. They decided the Torah and the prophets needed new explanations and applications as times were changing.

## UNDER THE GREEKS

And then everything changed for the Jewish people in 323 B.C. Alexander the Great died after conquering a huge swath of the globe. Two of Alexander's generals divided between themselves their conquered territories; General Ptolemy took Egypt in the south. General Seleucus made himself master of Syria in the north. Israel was in between. This would be the beginning of *two-and-a-half centuries* of horrific wars on Israel's soil. The atrocities between these two dynasties included annihilation of their own family members, intrigues, poisonings, murders, assassinations, and unimaginable massacres of huge proportions—and in between, conquering and reconquering the land of Judea over and over.

## JEWISH RABBIS TRANSLATE SCRIPTURES TO GREEK

At times, there were short periods of peace. Ptolemy the First carried thousands of Jews off to Egypt making them slaves. His son, Ptolemy II, freed them. Large populations of Jews settled in different areas of Egypt—especially the city of Alexandria (named after Alexander the Great). The younger generation of Jews soon spoke Greek, losing their Hebrew or Aramaic languages. To make the Word of God accessible to the Greek-speaking Jewish community, seventy Rabbis are said to have translated the Hebrew Biblical text into Greek.[6] That translation would come to be known as the Septuagint (meaning 70). They started with the Torah, and over the years, the rest of the Hebrew Bible was translated into Greek.

The Jewish people used this translation until the destruction of the Temple in 70 A.D. Since the New Testament was also written in Greek, many of its authors quoted Old Testament Scriptures from the Septuagint.

However, as Christianity among the Gentiles began to grow, the Septuagint became tagged as a "Christian book," and Jewish leaders decided to revert to the Hebrew text only.

## THE HELLENIZING OF THE JEWS

Meanwhile, the two warring dynasties of Ptolemy and Seleucus were united in one particular conviction. These power-crazed conquering generals and their progeny were determined to impose the Greek culture upon all the races and nationalities they governed. That, of course, included their gods. Many of the Jewish aristocratic elitists, including Israel's high priests, were receptive to the sophisticated and glamorous Greek lifestyle. The common people, on the other hand, wanted to cling to the Law of Moses.

But one of the Seleucid rulers, Antiochus Epiphanes, was determined to eradicate all signs of Judaism from the entire Jewish people. He converted the Temple into a sanctuary of Jupiter. He placed a statue of Jupiter on the altar. Heathen sacrifices were offered, and swine's blood was poured upon the altar, with the broth sprinkled all around the Temple. He also decreed it unlawful to keep the Sabbath and festivals. Torah scrolls were rent in pieces and burned. Children found to be circumcised were slaughtered, along with their mothers. All told, Antiochus murdered tens of thousands of Jews.

The liberalized Jews gave in. They were too worldly to be martyrs. On the other hand, the common folk were resigned to passive resistance. They presumed (from the Book of Daniel) the end of the world was at hand, and they just had to hold on until the Messiah appeared and set up his kingdom.

## AN OLD PRIEST AND HIS FIVE SONS

Instead, help came in the form of Judah the Maccabee, son of a priest named Mattathias who believed in active resistance. Judah and three of his brothers gave their lives fighting for freedom to believe in the Most High God, the Holy One of Israel. God gave him and his warriors success and three years later they rededicated the Temple. Some of the pious common people, called Hasideans (Hasidim in Hebrew), decided to join Judah's army. It is believed that these were the beginning of the Pharisees, who, at their conception, were strongly devoted to the Word of God.

The last of the living Maccabee sons, Simon, became the leader, backed by the emerging Roman Empire, and ruled a peaceful country for seven years. For a brief moment the Jews were free to practice the laws of their faith. However, Simon was granted the combined titles of "prince, commander and high priest forever" in 141 B.C., thanks to the Romans, vying for an entrance into the Greek's Middle East. But Simon's own Hasidim opposed him because no priest was also to become a king. The two titles were only to be given to the coming Messiah, from the tribe of Judah, according to the Scriptures.

Soon things went awry. Simon and his wife and family were murdered by his ambitious son-in-law, governor of Jericho. Simon's surviving son, Johanan Hyrcanus (135-104 B.C.) became totally immersed in the Greek lifestyle. He also designated himself as both high priest and head of the Jewish commonwealth.

From that time on, the priesthood became completely corrupt. High Priests gained their positions with money.[7]

## DISINTEGRATION OF TRUE WORSHIP

For the next hundred years, until the birth of Yeshua, there was continuous war, mass murders, scheming, and deception between the two Greek dynasties still fighting over the Holy Land, only to be ultimately defeated by the rising Roman Empire. The people were truly sheep without a shepherd. The elite, wealthy liberal Jews, including the High Priests, used Machiavellian cunning to curry favor from the latest foreign conqueror. The priestly rulers became known as Sadducees—who believed neither in heaven nor hell. Yet in religious matters they were rigidly observant, accepting as obligatory the Torah commandments. Nevertheless, morally, they were corrupt and worldly, with one thing in mind—power.

The Pharisees were hardly much better off. With no more godly prophets speaking the true words of God, the faith of the Pharisees' religion evolved into countless outward commandments and traditions, much of it created by themselves. They muddied the water with their feet, as Ezekiel warned.[8] By making fear the highest motive for the service of God, they busied themselves with minutiae. And they loved the accolades of the people who were in awe of their ostentatious display of piety. Except for a remnant, these leaders had forgotten what it meant to humbly serve God and to love Him with all their heart and soul and being, and to serve their fellow man. The Apostle Paul would write later, ***For I***

***bear them witness that they have a zeal for God, but not according to knowledge.*** *Romans 10:2 (NKJV)*

## THE WORD OF GOD APPEARS

By the time the Love of God appeared in the person of Yeshua, the Son of God, they had no idea who He was—the Word of God in the Flesh. They were no longer familiar with the *pure* Word of God; they had strayed so far with men's commandments they couldn't recognize Him.

From Israel's example, we see that extended times of turmoil and war do not always bring spiritual awakening to a people. In fact, they often bring out deep wickedness in men's hearts. It is active prayer and intercession that can maintain civil peace and freedom in a nation and allow the Kingdom of God to thrive.

> ***Therefore, I exhort first of all that supplications, prayers, intercessions, and giving of thanks be made for all men, for kings and all who are in authority, that we may lead a quiet and peaceable life in all godliness and reverence. For this is good and acceptable in the sight of God our Savior, who desires all men to be saved and to come to the knowledge of the truth.*** *I Timothy 2:1-4 (NKJV)*

Thankfully, there were many Jews who did recognize Yeshua when He came and took it upon themselves to share this Good News with the peoples of the earth.

The world can be ever grateful to those Jews who followed Him and gave their lives to the advancement of the Gospel.

No matter how dark the times, we have the promise from God that the Lord will bring the Jewish people back to Him when they recognize that Yeshua the Messiah is actually the Word of God that is the Son of God incarnate. The New Testament says, ***All Israel shall be saved, as it is written ...*** *Romans 11:26 (NKJV)*

When that day comes, God will pour out His Spirit on the whole world, giving them also the opportunity to be saved. And in the days of the Messiah's return, the pure Word of God will cover the earth!

> ***For out of Zion shall go forth the law, And the word of the Lord from Jerusalem.***
> *Isaiah 2:3b (NKJV)*
>
> ***For the earth will be filled with the knowledge of the glory of the Lord, As the waters cover the sea.*** *Habakkuk 2:14 (NKJV)*

## CHAPTER 3

*From the Apostles to the Reformation*

# WHEN THE WORD OF GOD CEASED TO EXIST

The Dark Ages of ignorance, poverty and abuse enshrouded the people of the Middle Ages, and the Word of God was hidden.

For 40 days after his death and resurrection, Yeshua the Messiah encouraged, energized and taught those closest to Him. Then He left for heaven. Exactly 10 days later, on the Jewish holiday of Shavuot (Pentecost), Yeshua sent the Holy Spirit in power to a gathering of 120 apostles and close associates of Yeshua who met on the second floor of someone's home.

That day 3,000 Jews believed in Yeshua and received salvation. The thousands multiplied as the disciples crisscrossed the land of Israel, bringing the Good News to their countrymen everywhere.

Then a vision of all kinds of non-kosher animals appeared to Peter, adding a new component foretold by the prophets, but hidden from the Jewish people until that moment. Gentiles were no longer to be considered non-kosher. The revelation to Peter was simply that every individual is created in the image of God and is valuable to God.

After all, the prophets had foretold that Israel was to be a light to the Gentiles. And before Yeshua ascended into heaven, He commanded His disciples to bring the Gospel to "every person in all the world."

Soon Paul, whose Hebrew name was Shaul, became the leader of the Jewish evangelists commissioned by God to reach the non-Jews. He began his ministry in Antioch, where the Gentile believers were first called Christians.

## APOSTLES SPREAD OUT TO EVANGELIZE WITH OLD TESTAMENT SCROLLS

Congregations of Jews and of Gentiles began to be planted around the known world. It is thought that Andrew went to Greece and Asia Minor. Tradition says Philip went to Hierapolis (Turkey) and archeologists recently claim they have found his tomb! Thomas was martyred in Persia or India. Judah is said to have evangelized in Armenia, Syria and Persia, where he, too, was martyred. Paul worked day and night for his Master, until he was most likely beheaded (usual punishment for a Roman citizen) in Rome around the time Peter was crucified.

The apostles had scrolls of the Old Testament in Greek as their source of Scripture. And with their personal first or second-hand witness of the risen Messiah, together with mighty miracles, they were seeing growing crowds of pagans receive everlasting life.

Realizing how important the written word was for the growth of believers in Yeshua, the apostles wrote 27 books, all in Greek, to add to the Old Testament. This collection would come to be known as the books of the New Covenant—or New Testament. Though few people could read, they received the Word of God through their leaders in their house meetings, and the Body of believers grew.

## COMMUNITY OF JEWISH BELIEVERS DISAPPEARS

For the first 40 years, the number of Yeshua's Jewish followers in Judea, Samaria and Galilee also grew, despite strong opposition of the Pharisees. But then, in 70 A.D. the Temple, Jerusalem, and for all practical purposes, the entire land of Israel was destroyed. Again, the Jewish people were exiled, this time by the Roman Legions.

Before that horrific event, the Jewish followers of Yeshua fled to Petra, according to a tradition cited by fourth century Christian historian, Eusebius. Whatever may have happened, the Jewish followers of Yeshua as a community disappeared.

Throughout the centuries, there would always be a remnant of Jews who followed Yeshua. Nevertheless, the commandment to make disciples would now almost completely be carried out by the growing non-Jewish community. This absence of a Jewish presence in spreading the Gospel would slowly result in the absence of their role in church influence and doctrine.

## EARLY FATHERS LEAD THE GROWING CHURCH

There are well-known fathers among the early Christians who faithfully shepherded the flocks of new Christians—men of faith like Clement of Rome and Polycarp of Smyrna—the latter is recorded to have been a disciple of the Apostle John.[9]

By the middle of the second century, however, the original disciples to the second and even third generation were gone. As the Gospel spread, the need arose for a version of the entire Bible in Latin (not just Greek), the language of the Roman Empire for the western regions of the empire.

## PERSECUTIONS OF EARLY CHRISTIANS

Beginning in 64 A.D., severe persecution began with Emperor Nero,[10] and continued off and on with terrible atrocities against church leaders and Christians until 311 A.D. Many of the Christian leaders were martyred—beheaded, crucified, burned or eaten alive by wild animals.

At times, whole communities were murdered. Even with all the persecution, the church grew. By the year 300, Christians accounted for approximately 10% of the Roman population—some six million Christians, according to estimates.[11]

From all reports, the great majority of Christians during the first 200 years were the real thing—including those who were later called popes and bishops. (It appears that leaders of Christian communities were called presbyters or bishops until somewhere around the middle of the second century, when the title "pope" in Rome was designated retroactively.)

## ANCIENT FRAGMENTS SHOW FEW VARIATIONS

During this time, countless numbers of scribes were copying the Word of God in Greek and Latin by hand, as the scrolls were distributed and shared from church to church. Then, around 320A.D., the codex book form replaced the roll or scroll, making it easier to read and transport. The Word of God was circulating freely among believers.

There exists today 5,800 early copies and fragments in Greek, the original language.[12] There are also another 8,000 in Latin. Moreover, there were scholars who translated the Bible into a few other languages, of which thousands of fragments remain. Most errors of these early manuscripts were misspellings and copy errors. Only one to two percent of the differences can be construed as real differences, and none of them have any impact on doctrine.

## EMPEROR BECOMES A CHRISTIAN

In the fourth century, everything changed. Christians saw the year 312 as a miracle year for the growing Gentile Church. The Emperor Constantine had a vision that transformed his life. Christianity became the dominant religion under the Emperor of the entire Roman Empire. Ten years later, he declared it the state religion. Persecution had come to a halt.

Indeed, it is recorded that Constantine commissioned the historian Eusebius to deliver fifty Bibles to the growing number of churches in Constantinople. He was serious about the Bible. Producing New Testaments and Bibles began in earnest—even though, we must remember, copying an entire Bible was still a huge undertaking. However, with this copying and translation activity over the next hundred years, confusing variations of Scripture texts in Latin began to circulate throughout the early church. The great fifth century scholar, Jerome, who had a passion to get the pure and accurate Word of God into the hands of the people wrote, “Ignorance of the scriptures is ignorance of Christ.”

Jerome was commissioned by the pope to translate an official definitive Latin version, using the earliest copies. In his monastery in Bethlehem, he authored what is called the *Vulgate*, finished in 405.[13] This became the official Bible used in Catholic churches to this day.

The work of copying the Scriptures continued to be undertaken in earnest in the monasteries of the early Middle Ages. Several thousand monasteries were established across Europe, and for many of the monks, making copies of the Scriptures was their chief task. They became the true guardians of the text and produced literally thousands of magnificent Bibles. Teams of scribes and artists worked with parchment to produce incredibly beautiful works of art. A scribe copying the Scriptures might use as many as 80 quills a day,[14] and artists embellished the work with intricate designs and illustrations.

Each Bible was made of sheep's hide. It took 250 sheep hides for the pages and thousands of hours to make one Bible.[15] In fact, a Catholic article states each Bible would be worth about $150,000 in today's economy. Churches actually chained their Latin Bibles to tables so they would not be stolen.

## WESTERN ROMAN EMPIRE COLLAPSES

Roman Emperor Constantine's support had given the Church new strength. But when he moved his capital from Rome to Byzantium (which he renamed Constantinople in his honor) the move created a power vacuum in Rome that was quickly filled by a formidable lineup of popes who created a kind of "papal monarchy." And then, in 476 A.D., the Roman Empire in the west completely collapsed from a Barbarian invasion.

The popes and the bishops appropriated not only religious, but also secular control over much of the old Roman world—with absolute governmental power to levy taxes, call up armies, make laws, and punish citizens who violated its laws.[16]

As the Roman Empire dissolved, multiple regional languages developed. Latin became a dead language. This, of course, meant huge populations no longer had access to the Scriptures in a language they could understand. Nevertheless, the Catholic Church continued to shepherd their flocks by conducting Mass in unintelligible Latin or Greek.

## CHURCH LITURGY REPLACES THE BIBLE

Over time, the Church began creating its own extra-biblical literature of its traditions and practices, and then placed it on the same level of authority as the Bible itself. (This is exactly what the leading rabbis did when recording their traditions and interpretations of the Bible called the Talmud and Gemara. They declared that these rabbinical books have the same authority as the Bible.)

Gradually, the doctrinal teachings of the Church replaced the Bible. Since most people couldn't read or write, the clergy was free to teach the Church's version of religion and practices, no matter how unbiblical they became. Encapsulated Bible and traditional stories were passed down in oral form that could be easily memorized. Stained-glass window pictures of the saints took the place of the Bible.

It became clear to the popes in Rome that their constituents should not be trying to read the Bible at all. And so the decrees went out in the sixth century that only the Latin Bible could be read.[17] Of course, nobody but highly-educated churchmen could read it. And the Church made sure its followers wouldn't read it in any other language. The pope and his bishops forbade the translation of the Bible into any of the vernacular languages. The light on the hilltop went dark.

## THE DARK AGES

For 1,000 years, Christians were not allowed to read a Bible in their mother tongue. This meant there were millions of Christians who had no direct access to the Bible.[18]

But it was even worse than that. Jerome's official Latin version (the *Vulgate*) had become corrupted with copiers inserting Catholic doctrine throughout the Scriptures they were copying.[19] In the ninth century, Emperor Charlemagne made a serious and extensive attempt to get the best scholars to return the *Vulgate* to its original form. But his efforts would not find wide distribution.

As centuries went by, even scholars were unable to discern the original Bible Scriptures from the interwoven Catholic teachings and interpretations.

## BIBLE PLUS

By the early fourteenth century, the condition of Jerome's *Vulgate* was deplorable with all its added notes.

Yet only a few of the most elite scholars were aware of it. It didn't really matter as, has been said, the majority of lay citizens couldn't understand it anyway. But just to make sure, in the thirteenth century, the pope proclaimed it illegal for lay members to even own a Bible in any other language, much less read one.

## CHRISTIANITY BECOMES PAGAN

Alongside the extreme lack of the Word of God among Christians was another debilitating and destructive force that had been at work for centuries. When Constantine declared the Roman Empire a Christian state, pagan gods and their traditions easily merged with Christianity.[20]

Since millions of Catholic Christians had no way of knowing what the pure Word of God said, the popes and their bishops decided for them. Anti-Semitism was one of the earliest signs of anti-Biblical doctrines that infiltrated and impregnated the Catholic Church.

The Scriptures had promised Abraham, ***I will bless those who bless you and whoever curses you I will curse.*** *Genesis 12:3 (NIV)* As the Church gained power, it became standard practice to publicly curse the Jews.

The renowned Church father, John Chrysostom, in the late fourth century delivered eight sermons of extreme violence against the Jews. To quote him: "The synagogue is not only a brothel and a theater; it is also a den of robbers and a lodging for wild beasts. No Jew adores God...

Jews are possessed by the devil; their debauchery and drunkenness gives them the manners of the pig ..."[21]

St. Augustine, the inimitable Catholic theologian, in his "Sermon against the Jews" declared that "though the [Jews] deserved the most severe punishment for having put Jesus to death, God kept them alive to be witnesses to the truth of Christianity."

Even Jerome, who translated the Vulgate Bible, described the Jews as "... serpents, wearing the image of Judas, their psalms and prayers are the braying of donkeys."[22]

That hatred of the Jewish people poisoned the faith of the early church. It clearly brought the curse of God on the church shepherds and their sheep as they cursed the children of Abraham. Sin and pride brought not only doctrinal error, but anti-Biblical behavior. In a sentence, the Catholic Church disintegrated into heresy and corruption.

Martyrs, once loved by their contemporaries, now became objects of veneration and worship. The people ceased praying to God in the Name of His Son, Jesus, and turned to praying to dead saints.

## HYPOCRISY FROM THE TOP

Although the papacy banned marriage among the clergy, the popes, bishops and a majority of priests openly displayed their mistresses, concubines, wives, illegitimate children and homosexual orgies.[23] They murdered, tortured and massacred their enemies. They created a hodgepodge of conflicting doctrines and ceremonies. Mary became the "Mother of God." Statues and images of saints became an integral part of their worship.[24] Christians just changed the names of their erstwhile pagan gods to those of the saints.

Power and mammon corrupted the leadership. They learned to enrich their pockets by enticing the well-to-do and the poor to pay cash for forgiveness of their sins and the sins of their relatives.

The popes sold ecclesiastical offices. Unqualified men purchased Church offices, enriching the coffers of the feudal lord or king. Does that sound familiar?[25] This is exactly the same practice that occurred during the late Maccabean period, when the wealthy Hellenistic Sadducees bought the offices of the High Priest and other important administrations.

No more evidence is needed to demonstrate that Gentiles could stray from the Narrow Path just as the Jews did. But for the grace of God, humanity always follows the same path toward power, greed and destruction.

The Dark Ages of ignorance and poverty and abuse enshrouded the people of the Middle Ages.

And the Word of God was hidden from them.

CHAPTER 4

*The Reformation and the Printing Press*

# THE BLOODY BATTLE TO LIBERATE THE WORD OF GOD

The sad truth is that when religious traditions ruled, the western world went dark. When the Word of God reappeared, nations rose to create the most advanced civilizations ever. Here is the story.

In the year 393 A.D., devout men of God studied the many manuscripts circulating among the churches. They were separating those writings they could certify as genuinely written by the original apostles of Yeshua from the unverifiable manuscripts. Only 27 books would be included in the New Testament. Certainly much research and prayer went into making such momentous historical decisions.

Even before the New Testament was formally completed as a book, it is documented that Emperor Constantine ordered 50 Greek Bibles to be distributed to the various growing churches in Constantinople, his capital. For a short time, the Word of God in Latin and Greek spread rapidly. But when the Roman Empire collapsed and Catholic Church leaders took over the government, freedom of religious belief and practices began to disappear. A secular *Huffington Post* journalist noted,

"Wouldn't you assume that the newly established Church [by Emperor Constantine] would have wanted its devotees to immerse themselves in the sanctioned New Testament, especially since the Church went to great lengths to eliminate competing Gospels? And wouldn't the best way of spreading the 'good news' be to ensure that every Christian had direct access to the Bible?"

The journalist continued: "That's not what happened. The Church actually discouraged the populace from reading the Bible on their own—a policy that intensified through the Middle Ages and later, with the addition of a prohibition forbidding translation of the Bible into native languages."

## EDUCATION FOR THE RICH ONLY

During the darkest of the Dark Ages, there were no schools for the poor; however, there was education in many cities and towns for the children of the rich. Oxford and Cambridge grew into universities in the 13th century. Universities existed in Italy, France and Germany—all of which taught Latin.

By the late Middle Ages, both religious and secular books were being copied and produced by professionals. Booksellers placed shops near the universities and cathedral schools, and so the book trade blossomed. For most people in the Middle Ages who were illiterate, picture Bibles full of wonderful illustrations became popular.

Because of the huge size of complete Bibles, they were divided into several volumes, and each was very costly. Only cathedrals, universities and the very rich could afford them.

Since so few could read and Bibles were incredibly expensive, the Roman Catholic authorities had long ago arrived at the conclusion that their parishioners really had little need to know the Scriptures themselves. But now this deprivation became law.

## STARVING THE SHEEP

So it was for nearly ten centuries that the Roman Catholic authorities, through their popes and their councils, forcibly took the Word of God from the sheep for which they had responsibility. In forbidding the Word of God, Roman Catholics (who condemned the Jews for their behavior historically) proved that the actions of the Christian leaders were no different than those of the ancient Jewish leaders. The disposition of the powerful towards more control and more corruption was simply human nature. They did not feed the sheep. The Roman Catholics were committing the same sin of which the prophets had accused the Jewish leaders in bygone times.

As the centuries passed, the domination and control over the people of Europe and everywhere the Church ruled became more extreme. To translate the Bible into one of the local languages became a crime that could cost a scholar his life—by the sword of the Roman Catholic Church.

> *Decree of the Council of Toulouse (1229 C.E.):* ***"We prohibit also that the laity should be permitted to have the books of the [Latin] Old or New Testament; but we most strictly forbid their having any translation of these books."***
>
> *Ruling of the Council of Tarragona of 1234 C.E.:* ***"No one may possess the books of the Old and New Testaments in the Romance language, and if anyone possesses them he must turn them over to the local bishop within eight days after promulgation of this decree, so that they may be burned ..."***

With the Word of God forcibly seized from citizens by the authorities with strict regulations to eliminate "heretics," and forbid the translation of the Bible into the peoples' mother tongues, sin dominated the Church, starting with the leaders and infiltrating the Christian world.

## A COURAGEOUS VOICE ARISES

But there was always an underground movement yearning to read the Bible. Many attempts were made to translate the Bible into different languages, but the translators were hunted down by the Church and punished as heretics. Even in the 10th century, a Bible scholar who actually managed to remain anonymous, dared to put the Gospels into English. But he could only circulate it privately because it was forbidden throughout Christendom.

Still others in different European countries tried secretly to translate portions of the Bible. Peter Waldo commissioned a translation in French—considered the first 'modern tongue' outside of Latin.[26] The Church excommunicated him in 1184.

His followers, called Waldensians, branched out all over Europe and waged an underground campaign to get the Bible to the people. For centuries, the Church launched an endless inquisition to stop their preaching and handing out Bibles; the group was nearly annihilated in the 17th century.

A few Waldensians escaped to France, Spain and Germany. Influenced by them, citizens of these countries joined together in the 13th and 14th centuries to demand complete Bibles in their own languages.

As Providence would have it, the vernacular languages in Europe now had enough fluidity, precision, breadth of word choice and beauty to support great and memorable versions of Scripture in the people's native languages.

## JOHN WYCLIFFE 1328—1384

On the stage appeared a great revolutionary, John Wycliffe, whose central doctrine was, *"Every Christian ought to study this book because it is the whole truth!"* He was a professor and theologian from Oxford University and the first to translate the New Testament into English to "*... helpeth Christian men to study the Gospel in that tongue in which they know best Christ's sentence.*"[27]

The Church condemned Wycliffe, but Oxford University shielded him from arrest. Wycliffe lashed out against the power and riches of the Church establishment and became an immensely popular leader at Oxford. As a renowned theologian, he was called in to advise parliament in its negotiations with the pope.

This was a world in which the Church was all-powerful, and the more contact Wycliffe had with Rome, the more indignant he became. The papacy, he believed, reeked of corruption and self-interest and he was determined to do something about it.

Wycliffe passionately believed the Bible should be available to everybody. He saw literacy as the key to the emancipation of the poor.

Inevitably, because of pressure from the papacy, he was condemned by the Archbishop of Canterbury and was fired from Oxford. However, his conviction of the authority of the Bible rather than the pope stirred great controversy.

He continued working on the translation of the whole Bible into English, and though he died three years later, his group of scholars finished the entire Bible in 1395. Despite the Church's efforts to suppress the Bibles, the common people were at last beginning to have an opportunity to read God's Word.

For this "heresy" Wycliffe was posthumously condemned by Arundel, the Archbishop of Canterbury. By the Council's decree "Wycliffe's bones were exhumed and publicly burned, and the ashes were thrown into the Swift River."[28]

## JAN HUS 1372—1415

At the same time, there were other educated men of God raising their voices in different areas of Europe, demanding the people receive a Bible in their own language. They paid with their lives.

Jan Hus was a Czech theologian from the University in Prague. He is considered the second most influential church reformer after John Wycliffe. He was ordained and became a preacher in Bohemia. He underwent a life change when he discovered the Bible. He testified that he left behind stupidity and foolishness *"when the Lord gave me knowledge of Scriptures."*

The writings of John Wycliffe had stirred his interest in the Bible. He wanted to place more emphasis on the Bible. Becoming a reformer, he proposed expanding the authority of local church councils—which meant lessening the power of the pope! He was driven to clean up the moral decay of the clergy. He began preaching such ideas as trusting in the Scriptures, *"desiring to hold, believe, and assert whatever is contained in them as long as I have breath in me."*

Meanwhile, at this time there were three elected popes, each claiming they were the legitimate pontiff. One of the three popes excommunicated Hus and forbade him to preach. Seeing the utter moral decadence of the papacy, including the accursed indulgences trafficked by the popes to fill their treasury, Hus leaned even more heavily on the Bible, proclaiming it the final authority for the Church.

He spent two years feverishly composing several treatises, one entitled "The Church." In it he argued that *"Christ alone is head of the church ... and to rebel against an erring pope is to obey Christ."*[29]

In November 1414, the Council of Constance assembled, and Hus was brought before a kangaroo court which sentenced him to death. His response:

*"I appeal to Jesus Christ, the only judge who is almighty and completely just. In his hands I plead my cause, not on the basis of false witnesses and erring councils, but on truth and justice."*

He was burned at the stake in 1415, his ashes tossed into a lake so that nothing would remain of the "heretic."[30] Out of those ashes arose a strong Bible-based movement, the Moravian Brethren, who sent many hundreds of missionaries around the world and played an influential role in the conversion of the Wesley brothers, among others. In fact, the Moravian missionaries were the first large-scale Protestant missionary movement, and remains a denomination today.

## GUTENBERG PRESS—1450

In the fullness of time, the greatest tool for spreading the Word of God since the Bible was written was invented! It surely was a gift the angels in heaven had been waiting for! The Gutenberg printing press went into operation in the year 1450. Within four years, the first Bible was printed. It was none other than the *Vulgate* Roman Catholic Bible in Latin—because still, it was mainly the rich and elite who could read, and the *Vulgate* was the only Bible widely known. But the Gutenberg printing press brought one of the greatest shifts for all mankind. It was the catalyst that birthed a renewal of true faith in God, the advancement of education and unprecedented prosperity.

The printing press would quickly become the Roman Catholic Church's greatest enemy, because soon Bibles were being printed much faster than the Church could burn them. Indeed, the printing press became a catalyst within the Roman Catholic Church itself, whether desired or not, to slowly break the chains of imprisonment of the Bible to its own members.[31]

But the war over the free usage of the Word of God in every language was far from over.

## CHAPTER 5

*The Word Comes to the German People*

# The Steep Price for a Bible You Could Actually Afford

The Dark Ages were not called dark for nothing. Most humans existed as slaves under another name. Eighty to ninety percent of Europe's population were serfs who worked for their masters or "lords," growing their food, raising their livestock, milling their grain and spinning their thread. They and their lords lived in virtually self-contained economic manors.

After their forced-labor duties were done, the peasants and their serf-born children then paid a hefty fee in exchange for using a piece of their master's land to eke out a few crops for their own survival. They could never leave their manor. They were completely illiterate, though their lord and his children probably had some education.

The Crusades had come and gone. The Popes had called for their mighty hordes of Crusaders to defeat the Muslims. Instead, they viciously slaughtered Jews and other minor Christian sects while failing to oust the Muslims.

Of course, Crusaders did learn and advance from their contact with the Muslims—like the numeric system we use today (1, 2, 3, 4), science, astronomy and even ship building, which added value to the wealthy and powerful of Europe.

But Europe's knowledge of God as written in the Bible had hit bottom. The religion they knew was to pray to Mary and the Saints and to pay money to the local priest to have their sins forgiven (indulgences). A personal relationship with their Savior, Jesus Christ, was forgotten, long ago, by the Roman Catholic Church.

## THE BLACK DEATH

Then the Bubonic Plague transformed Europe forever. In 1346, diseased fleas, riding on rats aboard ships, began to kill sailors. Wherever these ships docked and transferred goods onto horses, the fleas and the infected rats rode with them. The plague hit the entire continent. Twenty-two days after exposure, masses of people would die.

The living dug deep pits which, within a day, would be filled. The latest researchers say within seven years, 50 million Europeans died—60% of Europe.[32] This is a truly mind-boggling statistic. But the number of deaths around the world may have reached up to 200 million. Of course, no one knew what was causing the plague. Jews were accused of poisoning the wells, and thousands of them were burned at the stake by their countrymen.

What good could have come from the Black Death? Inevitably it had an enormous impact on European society and greatly affected the development of western civilization. So many serfs (and their masters) died that the entire economic order of western civilization was disrupted. There were no longer enough workers to till the land. Property changed hands. Many peasants, for the first time in centuries, began moving around, finding work with better conditions. Wages rose. Some were able to buy land for themselves or begin small businesses. Once again the European economy began to flourish and expand.

## YET ANOTHER CATASTROPHE

Still another disaster: The Byzantine Empire imploded from inside—as empires tend to do because of civil wars and struggles by their own greed-driven rulers. In 1453 a weakened Constantinople was overrun by the Ottoman Turks ending its 1,000-year reign.

Incredibly, even the fall of the Byzantine empire in 1453 helped fuel a budding Renaissance of education in Europe which would rediscover classical philosophy, literature and art. Even though the Renaissance was primarily a cultural movement which promoted humanism, it also helped lay the foundation for the Protestant Reformation.[33]

No one could have written a script that foresaw what was about to happen. In the Byzantine empire, Greek was still widely spoken by the elite, and students received education in Greek history and literature. There was also some Hebrew language scholarship, mainly among Jews. When the Ottoman Turks captured Constantinople, Greek scholars and Hebrew rabbis fled and brought their knowledge to Europe.[34] So both Greek and Hebrew were resurrected by European scholars' growing interest in these ancient languages. And the printing press had just been invented which would spread education throughout western Europe.

## MARTIN LUTHER 1483—1546

Just at this auspicious moment in time, a man appeared on the horizon who radically reshaped Germany's religion, language and culture. In fact, he fundamentally transformed western civilization. Ordained a priest in 1507, Martin Luther became a German professor of theology, composer, priest and monk—and a reformer. Like the Czech martyr John Hus, he especially despised the practice of indulgences to pay one's way out of hell.

As he studied the Bible, he concluded that salvation and eternal life are not earned by good deeds, but are a free gift of God's grace through faith in Jesus Christ as redeemer from sin. He challenged the Popes' authority by teaching that the Bible is the only source of divinely revealed knowledge.

Luther's goal was to equip every German-speaking Christian with the ability to read or hear the Word of God, and his translation of the Old and New Testaments from the original Hebrew and Greek into the vernacular by 1534 actually launched the Reformation.

His translation of the Bible into German had a tremendous impact on German culture. Besides challenging the Roman Catholic Church, it helped standardize the German language itself. His hymns influenced the development of singing in Protestant churches. His marriage to Katharina von Bora, a former nun, set a model for the practice of clerical marriage, allowing Protestant clergy to marry.

His *Ninety-five Theses,* which he posted on the door of All Saints' Church in 1517, sparked the Protestant Reformation. The Christian Church was ever after divided, and the Protestantism that soon emerged was shaped by Luther's ideas. His writings changed the course of religious and cultural history in the West.[35]

## PEOPLE LEARN TO READ

His New Testament was disseminated so quickly by printers that even tailors and shoemakers, yes, even women and ignorant persons who had accepted this new Lutheran Gospel and could read a little German, studied it with the greatest fervor as the fountain of all truth!

Though declared a heretic and his articles burned by the Catholic Church, he escaped execution because of his popularity with the common people. A local ruler who was an admirer "kidnapped" him and whisked him away to be hidden in a castle. It was there he began work on translating the entire Bible. In all, it took him ten years to finish his translation from Hebrew and Greek.

The precedent he set was followed by other scholars, whose work made the Bible widely available in different languages and contributed significantly to the development of those national languages.

However, in his later years, he seemed to become a bitter old man. His rage against Jews is an inerasable evil stain on his life and his accomplishments. His life is a warning to all of us that although a person can be mightily used by God to change a nation, hatred and rage, as was found in Luther, defiled an entire people and poisoned Christianity until Adolph Hitler found succor in Luther's writings. Nevertheless, it must be added: there had been a toxic malignancy of anti-Semitism throughout all the generations of the Roman Catholic Church. Though Luther was able to break away from much of the corruption of the Catholic Church, he was not able to shed this great sin.[36]

## CHAPTER 6

*William Tyndale 1494-1536*

# The Bible Translated into English

The English Reformation was bloodier than that of Germany. After John Wycliffe was vilified for translating the Bible into English near the end of the 1300's, the Roman Catholic Church decreed the death penalty for anyone found with an English Bible.

William Tyndale was studying at Oxford and Cambridge Universities where Wycliffe had also attended a hundred years earlier. For those working on a degree in theology, their textbook was the Latin *Vulgate* Bible, as no other language was allowed. The king during that period was the tyrant Henry VIII, a strong Catholic at the time.

But the halls of Cambridge were already flooded with Luther's ideas. Tyndale loudly complained,

*"They have decided that no man shall look at scripture, until he is nursed by heathen learning for eight or nine years and armed with false principles, which clean shut him out of the understanding of scripture."*[37]

Now William Tyndale's burning desire was to make the Bible available to all the common people of England. Shocked at the lack of elementary knowledge of the Bible even among the clergy, he told one priest,

*"I defy the pope and all his laws," replied William, "and if God spares my life, before many years pass I will help the boy who drives a plow to know more of the scriptures than you do!"*[38]

He went to London to ask the Bishop if he could be authorized to make an English translation of the Bible. The answer was no! So he left for Germany. He knew, of course, that John Wycliffe had created such a translation many years before, but his version was hand-copied, inaccurate, and extremely hard to find. Furthermore, it was translated from the Latin *Vulgate,* not from the original Hebrew and Greek.

## RISKING HIS LIFE

In Hamburg, Tyndale worked to finish an English translation of the New Testament, and in Cologne, he found a printer who would dare to print his work. However, news of Tyndale's New Testament got out and the press was raided. Tyndale escaped with the pages already printed and found another publisher in the city of Worms. Six thousand copies were printed and smuggled into England. The archbishop of Canterbury bought up copies from a friend of Tyndale and destroyed them. The friend then gave the money to Tyndale which he used to print an improved edition![39]

Tyndale had every reason to fear the Church's wrath. Only a few years before, six men and a woman were burned to death for teaching their children the Lord's Prayer and a few other verses in English, rather than Latin.[40] So Tyndale began translation of the Old Testament as he hid among the merchants in Antwerp while Henry VIII, the Pope and the Holy Roman Emperor were searching all over England and Europe for him.

## A TRUE GENIUS

He worked directly from the original Hebrew and Greek while comparing his work to the Latin *Vulgate* and Luther's recent German translation. He had learned Hebrew from rabbis he studied under in Germany. As for the Greek, he essentially taught himself! The style of his translation was simple and beautiful, words suitable for the common people. The *British Telegraph* newspaper recently wrote that his genius matched that of Shakespeare.

> ***In the beginnynge was the worde, and the worde was with God: and the worde was God.***
> *John 1:1*

He was eventually betrayed by an Englishman who pretended to be his friend, but then turned him over to the authorities. He was brought to trial for heresy—for believing, among other things, that the mercy offered in the Gospel was enough for salvation and forgiveness of sins. Some of the many charges were:

- He maintains faith alone justifies.
- He denies there is any purgatory.
- He affirms neither the Virgin nor the saints should be invoked by us.[41]

In 1536 he was condemned, and soon after was strangled and his body burned at the stake. The *Foxe Book of Martyrs* relates, "William said nothing for some time, then uttered a few final words: *'Lord, open the King of England's eyes.'*"[42]

## GOD HEARS THE CRIES OF MARTYRS

The harassment and execution of Bible-believing Christians droned on by the popes and Catholic royals throughout the 16th century. Then, by a series of flukes, England's famous King Henry VIII threw out the Catholic Church and its papal control and declared himself the head of the new Church of England (which would become known as the Anglican Church). He did this because the pope wouldn't allow him to divorce his wife who was not able to bear him an heir to the throne.[43]

Amazingly, that same year King Henry VIII made a complete U-turn and declared it legal to translate the Bible into English. He announced the power of the Roman Catholic Church would now be his. Two years later, he required every church in England to make a copy of the English Bible available to its parishioners!

To meet this demand, an English *'Great Bible'* (so-called because of its size) was put into production. It was based on William Tyndale's illegally translated version—as much as he was able to do before his death—and finished by Miles Coverdale in 1535. It was the first Bible to be printed in English from the original languages. Immediately 9,000 Bibles were distributed around England at the command of the Crown.[44]

Not surprisingly, all the shameless control and utter corruption of the Roman Catholic Church was swiftly transferred to the royal leadership of the newly created Anglican Church. When a group called the Pilgrims saw little improvement in doctrine and deeds, they continued to gather in secret to worship according to their understanding of the Bible.

## BACK TO CATHOLICISM

When King Henry VIII's daughter, Mary Tudor (called Bloody Mary), became queen in 1553, she was determined to return England back to the Roman Church. She burned at the stake 280 Protestant opponents, including John Rogers, the publisher of the Great Bible. Another 800 scholars fled to the Continent. Many of them went to Geneva and studied under John Calvin.

It was these Biblical scholars who eventually published the very first English version which included the Old

Testament translated entirely from Hebrew. Called the Geneva Bible, it was printed in the year 1560— some 50 years before the *King James Version.*[46] Almost no one has heard of this Bible today, but for generations it was popular among many Protestants, including the Pilgrims.

Fortunately, Queen Mary's royal rage against an English Bible was limited to a reign of five years, and her hopes for a Catholic England died with her.

In 1604, King James I, son of Mary Queen of Scots, united Scotland and England, and, as a Protestant, commissioned 47 scholars to produce the *King James Bible.* It was published in 1611. One estimate suggests the New Testament in the *King James* Version is 83% Tyndale's and the Old Testament 76%. In 2002, William Tyndale was placed at number 26 in the BBC's poll of the 100 Greatest Britons.

So why did a British king call for another new English translation when one had just been recently finished? King James I was offended by the commentary notes printed alongside the Scripture verses in the Calvin-influenced *Geneva Bible;* they taught that the Law of God ruled over the king! God, not the king, was supreme! King James I wanted a version without those notes.[47]

Indeed, despite his tainted motives, the king would prove the inevitability of God's word:

***Surely the wrath of man shall praise you.*** *Psalm 76:10 (NKJV)*

For the king's scholars would go on to translate what would become the most widely-read English version of all time—the *King James Bible.*

# CHAPTER 7

*Pilgrims Searching for Freedom*

# THE BIBLE ARRIVES IN THE AMERICAS

In the year 1620, 102 Pilgrims boarded the Mayflower ship and sailed to the Americas with their Geneva Bibles in search of a land where they could worship God according to the words of the Bible.[48] Only 52 survived the first winter. Their faith sustained them, although they could not have imagined the greatness of the nation they were birthing.

As the population in the New World grew, more Bibles were needed. Although one immigrant brought a primitive press from England in 1638, there was no press in America that could print a Bible. The one exception was a printing of the "Bay Psalm Book," a formidable achievement under the worst conditions.[49] Furthermore, believe it or not, according to British law, English Bibles could be printed only in England. New immigrants brought their

King James Bibles with them, which became the preferred version.

The printing of the first full Bible in the New World is so symbolic of America's great exceptionalism. The very first printed Bible in America was John Eliot's *Algonquin Indian language Bible,* printed in 1663 on that same crude wooden press.[50] He spent the rest of his life dedicated to serving as a missionary to the native people. He believed the indigenous population should be able to read the Bible in their own language.

But as conflict grew between Britain and the colonies, the flow of immigrants and trade, including Bibles to the New World, came to a halt. The Word of God became precious in the colonies. Then a Scottish immigrant to Philadelphia, Robert Aiken, dared to print a New Testament in 1777, breaking Britain's monopoly on printing English Bibles. It would be 160 years after the arrival of the *Mayflower* that Aiken printed the first *King James Bible* called *"The Bible of the Revolution,"* authorized by an act of Congress on September 12, 1782.

Many years ago, my university professor told us how the early English and European pioneers who arrived in the New World were searching for a place where they could freely worship God. With that foundation, America, until now, has become the most prosperous nation in the history of mankind. In contrast, South American nations were founded by Spanish and Portuguese conquistadores who were hunting for gold. Most of these nations have suffered centuries of great poverty and crime and little access to the Bible in their languages.

The Roman Catholic Church has dominated these nations, and wherever it has had the upper hand, it fought a continuous bitter war against Protestants and their "local language" Bibles. In fact, until the 20th century, the Latin *Vulgate* (a long-dead language) was the only translation the Catholic church would permit.[51]

But God has not forgotten the people of the Spanish and Portuguese languages. In the last few decades, many nations in South America are experiencing great revival and incredible growth in evangelical and Pentecostal churches. They are shaking off the shackles of a religion that, until recently, continued to discourage their members from reading the Bible.

## CHARISMATIC RENEWAL IN THE CATHOLIC CHURCH

It would be incomplete on my part not to note some significant, yes, massive changes within the Roman Catholic Church over the last 50 plus years. Though the present pope is a confirmed liberal, millions of their members are experiencing an intimate born-again relationship with Jesus, as they regularly read and study the pure Word of God. The Holy Spirit is moving to bring both Renewal and Revival in the Roman Catholic Church.[52]

They are testifying that because of their love of Scripture, evangelical Catholics are discovering a new love for the

Jewish people. Indeed, in 1965 the Church officially repudiated Replacement Theology that had dominated its teachings for centuries.

My Irish Catholic friend, who is a strong Evangelical believer and leader within the Evangelical Catholic movement, believes his Church's repentance of replacement (or supersessionist) theology ushered in the move of the Holy Spirit in 1967, speaking in new languages, much like what happened in the Book of Acts.

(As an aside, my friend asked if there is any other Church body or denomination that I know of that has *officially* repented of Replacement Theology. Alas. I know of none.)

The Catholic News Agency estimated there were some 160 million Charismatic Renewal members in 2014.[53] I myself was present at Notre Dame when the power of the Holy Spirit was poured out in 1967. I can affirm there was a mighty presence of the Holy Spirit as Catholics testified of their new relationship with Jesus Christ and being filled with the Holy Spirit.

## PROTESTANTS CONSUMED WITH GETTING THE BIBLE INTO EVERY LANGUAGE

As for Protestants, from the 1800's on, translating the Bible into other languages became a full-fledged passion—especially in English-speaking countries. In that century, 400 new language groups received a translation—including the first Chinese Bible. (A more accurate

Chinese Bible was finished in 1992.) More recently, in the first 50 years of Wycliffe Bible Translators' existence, they were able to translate the Bible into 500 languages. The second 500 translations took only 17 years!

Today, the Bible is the most translated book in the world. Still, there is so much more work to do. At present, there are over 7,000 languages in the world. But one truth unifies these translators: translation of Bibles into new languages is seen as crucial to spreading the Word of God and fulfilling the Great Commission.

It just so happens that in the 21st century, technology to translate the Bible has changed the world far beyond the scale of the printing press in the 1400's. Man will now be able to translate and publish the Bible in literally every language and tongue in the world over the next few years through digital printing and the Internet!

## GOAL: TO HAVE THE BIBLE IN EVERY LANGUAGE BY 2033

In 2010, one of the most important meetings in the history of the world took place. Ten of the largest Bible translation agencies came together to determine how they could eradicate "Bible poverty" from the world. Out of that meeting came the "Every Tribe Every Nation" (ETEN) alliance where they all agreed to pool their resources and collaborate with the goal of having at least a portion of Scripture translated in every living language by the year 2033![54]

Their aim is to produce enough Scripture in each language so the message of salvation will be clear. Together with more than 500 years of collective experience, these ten organizations began translating and publishing Bibles with exponential speed.

The plans to finish this monumental task in our generation is quickly progressing. They have chosen to put aside their egos and logos to meet this goal. Their collaboration makes sure there is no duplication of projects among the agencies, and they are sharing data, languages and techniques for the quickest and most accurate translations.

Technology now aids virtually every step of Bible translation. Where translations once took even decades to complete, advancements in technology have made it possible to translate new languages in a fraction of the time. Now through a Digital Bible Library, the Bible agencies have uploaded over 2,100 versions of the Bible, free to over six billion people![55]

## TECHNOLOGY WILL BRING GOD'S WORD TO THE ENTIRE HUMAN RACE

But God has more technology just around the corner to get His Word out to the world. One of several plans to supply high speed internet to the globe's poorest is a creation of Elon Musk, CEO of SpaceX. He has announced he has plans to launch thousands of satellites about 340 miles above the earth's surface to create the largest broadband network ever.[56]

Whatever Musk's primary purposes may be for this network, his or some other company's technology will make access to the Bible possible from any machine in the world that can connect to the Internet.

Since the Protestant Reformation, it is estimated that over six billion Bibles have been printed, with a hundred million hard-copy new Bibles sold yearly!

My brother, Gilbert Lindsay, has been printing Bibles in Belarus for three decades. He arrived in Minsk in November 1990, a year before the Iron Curtain fell. Miraculously, he was allowed to stay. Over the last 30 years, Gilbert has printed 30 to 40 million Bibles for 115 countries in approximately 100 languages.

When I talked to him recently, he had just shipped 80,000 Bibles to South Sudan—one of the most desolate and dangerous countries in the world. At the moment he is working on orders in these languages: Polish, French, Chinese, Bulgarian, Laotian, Asang Khongca, Thai and Spanish, including a shipment to the stricken nation of Venezuela. In fact, he has just sent one million complete Bibles to Papua New Guinea to be used in their schools!

## A PROPHETIC NEW YORK TIMES?

There is still one more ingredient to complete this story. A sign. A miracle. A marvel of God's handiwork in these end times. I found it in the *New York Times,* of all places. Obviously, they had no clue they were writing prophetically in this front-page article that said:

> "A half century ago, a majority of the world's people had always been illiterate; now we are approaching 90 percent adult literacy. There have been particularly large gains in girls' education—and few forces change the world so much as education and the empowerment of women. In this 21st century, there has been elimination of diseases, illiteracy and the most extreme poverty.
>
> "Just sixty years ago, a majority of the world's population had always been illiterate and lived in extreme poverty. Within a couple of decades, illiteracy and extreme poverty may be almost completely eliminated."
> *New York Times*, Dec. 30, 2019

Do we see yet one more sign that the coming of the Lord is near? Here it is: John the Apostle in his vision of heaven saw the redeemed saints who were in heaven:

***"a great multitude that no one could count..."***

They were ***"from every nation, tribe, people and language, standing before the throne and before the Lamb."*** *Revelation 7:9 (NIV)*

God has ordained that within a generation virtually the entire world will be literate for the first time in history! Furthermore, He has given men and women the capacity to create a communication tool that reaches into the farthest corners of the earth.

And He has raised up heroic translators, dedicated to bringing the Bible to every single language group in the world.

The Scriptures foretell that when this Age ends, the Gospel will have reached every single nation, tribe, people and language. We're almost there!

## AND THEN THERE IS ISRAEL...

This challenge to publish the Bible in an easily understood format even exists in Israel today! Believe it or not, very few of God's chosen people, "the People of the Book," have access to the Word of God in a language they can understand.

Yes, the Old Testament is in Hebrew. But it is a very ancient Hebrew that is difficult to understand for the average Israeli, even if highly educated. Imagine if your only copy of this life-changing book was written in old Shakespearean or even Chaucer English.

Therefore, I conclude with deep gratitude and excitement that in coordination with the Israel Bible Society, and Maoz Israel Ministries, we have been able to play a small part in making sure no people group is left without a Bible they can understand—not even Israelis!

Yes, we have published in Hebrew the *Narrated Bible in Chronological Order* both the Old Testament and New Testament with many modern Hebrew helps! Of course, the Hebrew Scriptures of the Old Testament *will remain in their original ancient Hebrew.* Moreover, we are using the best New Testament *modern Hebrew translation* from the original Greek.

What makes this Bible so unique and revelatory is the many different "helps" we have included to make it the most readable Hebrew Bible ever published.

One of its most exciting features is that the entire Bible is arranged in chronological order!

Then with easy-to-understand narration introducing each portion, together with subtitles and a dictionary for hard words at the bottom of each page, it will enable countless Israelis to read and more easily understand the ancient Hebrew text for the first time in Israel's modern history.

**There are 7,353 Languages in the World as of 2020**[57]:

1 in 5 people—have no Bible

698 Languages—have the full Bible

1,548 Languages—have the New Testament

1,138 Languages—have some portion of the Bible

2,617 Languages (approx.)—in process of translation

1,800 Languages (approx.)—still need to begin translation

Our work still lies ahead of us! Let's be the generation that propels the Bible forward to every tribe, language, and people!

# SOURCE NOTES

At the time of publication, the following links/resources were active on the Internet:

[1] https://israelseen.com/israel-seen-oldest-alphabet-identified-as-hebrew/

[2] Exodus 12:37

[3] jbqnew.jewishbible.org

[4] II Kings 24:13-16, II Kings 25:11

[5] Jeremiah 52:30

[6] https://en.wikipedia.org/wiki/Septuagint

[7] https://blogs.timesofisrael.com/hanukahs-lesson-political-corruption-leads-to-jerusalems-temples-desecration/

[8] Ezekiel 34

[9] https://en.wikipedia.org/wiki/Polycarp

[10] http://www.bbc.co.uk/history/ancient/romans/christianityromanempire_article_01.shtml

[11] https://www.britannica.com/topic/Vulgate

[12] http://textusreceptusbibles.com/Is_Textual_Criticism_Relevant

[13] https://www.britannica.com/topic/Vulgate

[14] https://www.biblica.com/resources/bible-faqs/how-was-the-bible-distributed-before-the-printing-press-was-invented-in-1455/

[15] https://www.catholicbridge.com/catholic/did-the-catholic-church-forbid-bible-reading.php

[16] https://www.rome.net/papacy-rome

[17] https://en.wikipedia.org/wiki/Censorship_of_the_Bible

[18] https://journal.christianscience.com/shared/view/1s3lqjua7m8

[19] http://www.reformation.org/corrupt-latin-vulgate.html

[20] https://en.wikipedia.org/wiki/Religious_policies_of_Constantine_the_Great

[21] The Fathers of the Church St. John Chrysostom, Discourses against Judaizing Christians, Translated by Paul W. Harkins

[22] International Journal of Integrative Humanism Vol 11. No. 1, pg 40

[23] https://www.google.com/search?client=safari&rls=en&q=Medieval+church+corruption+brewminate&ie=UTF-8&oe=UTF-8

[24] https://carm.org/catholic/list-of-roman-catholic-false-teachings

[25] https://www.thirdmill.org/newfiles/jac_arnold/CH.Arnold.RMT.1.html

[26] https://en.wikipedia.org/wiki/Peter_Waldo

[27] https://www.wycliffe.org.uk/stories/john-wycliffe/

[28] https://en.wikipedia.org/wiki/John_Wycliffe

[29] https://deovivendiperchristum.wordpress.com/2013/10/30/jan-hus-c-1369-1415-christ-alone-is-the-head-of-the-church/

[30] https://www.britannica.com/event/Council-of-Constance

[31] https://www.christianitytoday.com/history/issues/issue-16/what-tyndale-owed-gutenberg.html

[32] https://www.historytoday.com/archive/black-death-greatest-catastrophe-ever

[33] https://dailyhistory.org/How_did_the_Renaissance_influence_the_Reformation%3F

[34] https://greekcitytimes.com/2020/05/29/on-this-day-may-29-1453-the-fall-of-constantinople/

[35] https://edition.cnn.com/2017/10/29/world/reformation-world-change/index.htm

[36] https://www.jewishvirtuallibrary.org/martin-luther-quot-the-jews-and-their-lies-quot

[37] https://www.plough.com/en/topics/faith/witness/william-tyndale

[38] http://www.william-tyndale.com/tyndale-bible-history.html

[39] https://www.christianity.com/church/church-history/timeline/1501-1600/translator-william-tyndale-strangled-and-burned-11629961.html

[40] William Tyndale: Did You Know, ChristianHistoryInstitute.org

[41] https://christianhistoryinstitute.org/magazine/article/tyndales-betrayal-and-death

[42] https://bible.org/seriespage/prologue-william-tyndale-father-english-bible

[43] https://www.history.com/news/henry-viii-divorce-reformation-catholic-church

[44] https://www.bl.uk/collection-items/the-great-bible-probably-henry-viiis-own-copy

[45] https://en.wikipedia.org/wiki/Mary_I_of_England

[46] https://www.biblegateway.com/versions/1599-Geneva-Bible-GNV/

[47] https://founders.org/2011/10/12/the-geneva-bible-and-its-influence-on-the-king-james-bible/

[48] https://digitalcommons.cedarville.edu/kjv_america/

[49] https://uh.edu/engines/epi733.htm

[50] https://www.christianity.com/wiki/bible/what-was-the-first-bible-printed-in-america.html

[51] Here is a link that lists a number of English Catholic translations of the Bible or parts of it from the 16th century. However there is little or no information as to whether the Church allowed its members to read them, or how widely they were distributed. https://maybetoday.org/scriptura/bible-in-english/catholic-bibles-a-modest-history-of-the-english-versions/#early

[52] https://www.youtube.com/watch?v=J-QDOcDGDWA&feature=youtu.be

[53] https://www.catholicnewsagency.com/news/brazil-catholic-community-leads-surging-charismatic-renewal-72952

[54] https://www.ugchristiannews.com/bible-to-be-translated-for-99-9-of-the-worlds-population-by-2033/

[55] https://outreachmagazine.com/features/global/42457-a-bible-for-every-language.html

[56] https://www.bloomberg.com/news/articles/2020-09-17/elon-musk-s-starlink-wants-to-beam-broadband-internet-from-40-000-satellites

[57] https://www.wycliffe.org.uk/resources/press-releases/latest-bible-translation-figures/

# MEET SHIRA SORKO-RAM!

As the daughter of Gordon and Freda Lindsay, founders of Christ for the Nations in Dallas, Texas, Shira was raised in a culture of missions and outreach.

Shira first visited Israel in 1959. After several trips to the Middle East, she permanently moved to Israel in 1967, and eventually became an Israeli citizen. From Eliezer Ben Yehuda's son—the man responsible for resurrecting Hebrew as a spoken language—to the first Prime Minister, Ben Gurion, Shira met several early leaders of modern Israel, and even became personal friends with some.

As a gifted and anointed film producer/director, she also won an audience with Prime Minister Golda Meir for her film ***"Dry Bones,"*** a widely-acclaimed documentary about the prophetic significance of Israel's rebirth.

Shira has written for many publications concerning the Messianic Jewish Movement and the part believing Christians will play in Israel's spiritual resurrection. For 45 years she wrote the monthly ***Maoz Israel Report,*** giving a prophetic, political, and spiritual perspective of current events in Israel.

Shira and her husband, Ari, founded Maoz Israel Ministries, leading it for over 40 years. During that time, they pioneered several Messianic Jewish congregations in the Tel Aviv area, sponsored national conferences for Israeli and Arab believers, and established a humanitarian fund called *I stand with Israel.*

They translated and published well-known books into Hebrew, encouraged and sponsored born-again Jews returning to Israel, helped immigrants with small businesses, supported Arab leaders who have a heart for evangelism and for Israel, and assisted in the fight for the civil rights of Jewish believers in Yeshua (Jesus) in the land of Israel. They passed the leadership of Maoz to **Kobi and Shani Ferguson,** their son-in-law and daughter, in January 2021.

Ari and Shira reside in the Tel Aviv area. They have two sabra (born in Israel) children, and six grandchildren.

TO ORDER MORE COPIES,
EMAIL: INFO@MAOZISRAEL.ORG

*Shira met many early leaders of Israel. In this photo she meets David Ben Gurion, Israel's first Prime Minister.*

**GAIN ACCESS TO A SELECTION OF SHIRA SORKO-RAM'S ARTICLES FROM THE *MAOZ ISRAEL REPORT,* SPANNING DECADES OF HER LIFE IN ISRAEL, AT WWW.MAOZISRAEL.ORG.**

Each month our friends and partners receive the *Maoz Israel Report*—a free publication written and produced in Israel. If it's not currently arriving in your own mailbox, we invite you to enjoy a personal copy.

You'll love the inspiring stories, get up-to-date information on Israel's current events from a prophetic, political, and spiritual perspective, and receive first-hand information and insight without the filter of western media. There's nothing else quite like it.

You'll also learn how you can personally get involved with Israel by supporting various projects that strengthen the Body of Believers in Israel and offer humanitarian aid to widows, orphans, the needy, oppressed and victims of terrorism in Israel.

Visit maozisrael.org and subscribe to receive the *Maoz Israel Report* and updates from Israel.

## SIGN UP AND GET CONNECTED!

Thank you for supporting our efforts as we bring the Good News of Messiah to the people of Israel until all Israel is saved!

> "I have been reading the Maoz Israel Report for years, and as far as I'm concerned it is the only newsletter I would read having to do with End Time Bible prophecy—right from Israel!"
>
> —*Sid Roth*